'Tis a Blessing to Be Irish

'Tis a Blessing to Be Irish

written by
Rosemary Purdy

illustrated by
R.W. Alley

One
Caring
Place

Abbey Press

Text © 2001 by Rosemary Purdy
Illustrations © 2001 by St. Meinrad Archabbey
Published by One Caring Place
Abbey Press
St. Meinrad, Indiana 47577

Library of Congress Catalog Number
00-109612

ISBN 0-87029-351-6

Printed in the United States of America

Foreword

Being Irish isn't something you do. It's something you are.

Being Irish means that your heart swells like a sheet on a clothesline at the sound of your ancestral brogue, that the thought of your da and sainted mother makes you weep a wee bit even now, that the devil himself, try as he does, will never dim your devotion to the Trinity.

Being Irish means you're possessed of a joy of spirit and a depth of soul. You carry a smile for a stranger and coins aplenty for the poor. Aye, there's a feistiness about you as well, but only in protecting all that you hold dear: family and friends, faith and land, your heritage.

For if you can see a masterpiece in a sunset and a promise of harvest in a clump of dirt, if you can claim friends who'll buoy you up as well as cheer you when you sail, if you can feel the loving grip of God whatever your lot in life, then saints be praised... you're Irish.

May this book and the wee folk herein help you to celebrate your Irish heritage with pride!

—Victoria Ryan

1.

You can tell you're Irish, not
by your looks or the county you
hail from, but by your character.
If you have a twinkle in your
eye, a song upon your lips,
a kind word on your tongue,
and two feet planted solidly on
the good earth—then, saints be
praised, you're Irish!

2.

Research your family tree. Your Irish ancestors are part of you—not only through the color of your eyes or the cast of your complexion, but also through your Irish spunk and spirit. Tracing the roots of your family tree will help you bring the past to life and nurture your sense of self.

3.

Explore Irish culture. Ask your relatives to tell you all they know about your family's Irish background—and life in the old country. Learn some Irish traditions, practices, and recipes, and adapt them for your own household.

4.

Cherish your kith and kin. Consider their happiness as your joy, their misfortune as your woe, twice over. An Irish family is an unbroken circle of strength and support, entwined with love. Keep your loved ones ever close at hearth and heart.

5.

"Two shorten the road," the Irish say, and a friend for the journey of life is a priceless treasure. A friend will walk the uphill road with you, in the face of a biting wind. A friend will bask with you in the contentment of cloudless skies. Be loyal to friendship.

6.

Remembering the trials and triumphs in their pursuit of freedom, Irish hearts are forever faithful to their country. Love your own country; be thankful for its beauty and bounty, its peace and privileges. Honor the sacrifices of your nation's patriots by never taking freedom for granted.

7.

The Irish love for land is legendary. Their land is their lot in life, their source of life and livelihood, their own piece of Paradise. Be close to the earth. Walk on it, dig in it, grow in it. *Stay grounded.*

8.

To be Irish is to be in love
with nature. A morning's
mist gilded with sunshine,
the springtime emerald of the
hills, the shimmer of a
sapphire lake—all will turn
an Irish heart to rapture.
Take time to appreciate the
wonders of nature.

9.

There is no day so dull or
dismal that it is not an
occasion for rejoicing.
Eat, drink, laugh, and be Irish.
Celebrate today!

10.

Whether it's the trill of a tin whistle, the twang of the fiddle, or the fluid melody of the harp, music never fails to move the Irish heart. Music is a proper accompaniment for every kind of celebration or any time at all. Sing, hum, play, or listen to some music today. It does a soul good.

11.

The Irish boast a proud tradition of dance, celebrated the world over, especially in recent years. Treat yourself to a live performance of Irish dancing. Consider every day wasted on which you do not dance at least once.

12.

In Ireland, the folks are so witty,
Each word that they utter is pretty.
There's no other folks
So quick with the jokes—
Or with poetry named for their city!

Indulge in some word play or
riddles. Try writing a limerick
in honor of a friend. Make
someone's day...Irish!

13.

The Irish joke about the serious and are serious about joking. Lighten up! Poke some fun at yourself, or share a rib-tickling joke. 'Tis a worthy deed to set others' hearts to gladness.

14.

Ever since St. Patrick used a shamrock to explain the Trinity, the Irish have lovingly kept and tended the Christian faith. Their faith is a bridge of trust connecting them with God, a promise of hope in hard times, a treasure at the rainbow's end. Keep the faith and pass it on.

15.

To the Irish, prayer is as natural and familiar as chatting with a neighbor over the stile. They pray about everything—their mortal soul (and that of their gossipy neighbor), rain for the crops, sunshine for the parade. Do likewise—have a good gab with God today.

16.

The lucky "coincidences" of our lives are really miracles for which God chooses to remain anonymous. And the "luck of the Irish" is actually the grace of God, acknowledged and appreciated. Look for the hand of God in the providential happenings in your own life.

17.

There are literally hundreds of Irish saints, both male and female. The Irish pray to them daily for direction and protection, and to intercede for them with Christ. Entrust a special intention to a saint whose life inspires you.

18.

Irish wakes are grand and lively celebrations, with plenty of food, drink, talk, and music. The Irish consider life and death as warp and weft of the same cloth. Celebrate the life on earth—and the life in heaven—of someone close to you who has died.

19.

The Irish are proud and humble, quick to laugh or weep, easygoing and stubborn, exuberant and brooding. This is not a paradox to be reconciled but, rather, evidence of a special depth of soul, which allows the Irish to experience the whole of life. Embrace all of life—the shadows and the light. Live deep!

20.

The Irish are children of the rainbow. Through famine, oppression, and war, they have always looked forward in hope to deliverance by the hand of God. Look for rainbows amidst the clouds in your life; cope through hope.

21.

The Irish always have an extra penny for the poor or a potato to halve with someone hungrier. Practice the Irish virtue of generosity by sharing your abundance with those less fortunate.

22.

God doesn't give us all we want, but surely all we need. And who needs more than a harvest that outlasts the winter, a good friend to share a "cuppa" tea, and a breath of thanks upon the lips? Live simply...Simply live.

23.

Irish hospitality means offering
every guest the same welcome
you would offer Christ himself.
Open heart and hearth in the
spirit of hospitality. A hundred
thousand welcomes are none too
many for the wayfarer at the
door.

24.

With eyes fixed on heaven, the Irish still enjoy the sensual delights of earthly existence: the lilt of a child's laughter, the warm caress of a flannel blanket on a chilly night, the hearty taste of a filling soup. Enjoy the sublime in life's little joys.

25.

An Irish temper is a spark that can cause good or ill. If you have inherited a fiery temper, learn to control its destructive power. Let it ignite your zeal in the service of good, such as leading a campaign against injustice.

26.

Giving someone an Irish blessing is like invoking God's "blanket protection" for life…and even beyond: "May your neighbors respect you, trouble neglect you, the angels protect you, and heaven accept you." Practice random acts of blessing.

27.

Beauty is the kiss of heaven upon the soul. Whatever beauty you experience becomes a part of you forever. Seek out beauty—the exquisitely crocheted doily or the pasture drenched in sunshine—and savor it.

28.

From the Celtic folktales, to the legends of St. Patrick, to the modern writings of James Joyce, Irish bards and poets have sustained a rich literature. Do your soul a kindness by reading from this wealth of words.

29.

Through the ages, imagination has lifted the Irish above life's toils and troubles to the realms of fairies, leprechauns, dragons, and mythic heroes. Indulge your Irish imagination. A flight of fantasy now and then provides a healthy balance to the daily grind.

30.

Use your Irish gift of gab and tell a story. Not only does a good yarn charm the listener, but it also captures the history and wisdom of the age for posterity. And, by the by, if the tale gets embroidered with a bit o' blarney—all the better!

31.

Ireland is "the one place on earth that heaven has kissed with melody, mirth, and meadow and mist." And it has an uncanny way of calling its own back to itself. Visit the Emerald Isle if you can. Bring back stories and pictures to show to those not fortunate enough to go.

32.

The ruins of Celtic crosses, towers, forts, and burial mounds are some of the most magnificent ancient monuments in Europe. Make an effort to visit these sites by book or in person to acquire a sense of the mighty influence of Celtic culture.

33.

Irish history is rich with noble ideals, heroic deeds, and the valiant quest for freedom. You have descended from a long line of Irish patriots. Let their stories inspire you to find and follow your own purpose in life.

34.

During the Dark Ages, Irish monks kept the light of learning alive. Recording oral tradition and copying the written knowledge of the time, they produced illuminated manuscripts that preserved the wisdom of Western civilization. Be thankful for the painstaking labors of these Irish scribes.

35.

Make St. Patrick's Day a special holiday in your home by eating traditional Irish foods. Watch a parade—or even join in with a jig—to show your Irish spirit. And don't forget that being Irish is something to celebrate 365 days of the year!

36.

The true legacy of an Irish heritage is love: love for the earth, love for life, love for God. Hold fast to this legacy and hand it down to the next generation.

37.

As they say in the old country:
If you're lucky enough to be
Irish, you're lucky enough. No
matter how far away you live,
no matter how distant your
Irish ancestors, Ireland will
always be part of you. Thank
the Good Lord.

38.

May you take deep pride in your
    Irish heritage.
May a friend be ever at
    your side.
May loved ones grace
    your hearth,
contentment warm your heart,
and, until you meet face-to-face,
may God hold you in the
    hollow of His hand.

Rosemary Purdy is a writer who is half Irish and half German—like many others whose ancestors settled in the Ohio River Valley. She does a respectable jig, has a touch of Irish in her complexion (and temper), and always serves green mashed potatoes to her family on St. Patrick's Day.

Illustrator for the Abbey Press Elf-help Books, **R.W. Alley** also illustrates and writes children's books. He lives in Barrington, Rhode Island, with his wife, daughter, and son.

The Story of the Abbey Press Elves

The engaging figures that populate the Abbey Press "elf-help" line of publications and products first appeared in 1987 on the pages of a small self-help book called *Be-good-to-yourself Therapy*. Shaped by the publishing staff's vision and defined in R.W. Alley's inventive illustrations, they lived out author Cherry Hartman's gentle, self-nurturing advice with charm, poignancy, and humor.

Reader response was so enthusiastic that more Elf-help Books were soon under way, a still-growing series that has inspired a line of related gift products.

The especially endearing character featured in the early books—sporting a cap with a mood-changing candle in its peak—has since been joined by a spirited female elf with flowers in her hair.

These two exuberant, sensitive, resourceful, kindhearted, lovable sprites, along with their lively elfin community, reveal what's truly important as they offer messages of joy and wonder, playfulness and co-creation, wholeness and serenity, the miracle of life and the mystery of God's love.

With wisdom and whimsy, these little creatures with long noses demonstrate the elf-help way to a rich and fulfilling life.

Elf-help Books

...adding "a little character" and a lot
of help to self-help reading!

Celebrate-your-womanhood Therapy	#20189
Acceptance Therapy (color edition) $5.95	#20182
Acceptance Therapy	#20190
Keeping-up-your-spirits Therapy	#20195
Slow-down Therapy	#20203
One-day-at-a-time Therapy	#20204
Prayer Therapy	#20206
Be-good-to-your-marriage Therapy	#20205
Be-good-to-yourself Therapy (hardcover) $10.95	#20196
Be-good-to-yourself Therapy	#20255